THE 5 AM REVOLUTION

B. VINCENT

THE 5 AM REVOLUTION

UNLOCKING YOUR
POTENTIAL ONE MORNING
AT A TIME

QuillQuest Publishers

CONTENTS

First Printing, 2024

CHAPTER 1: LAYING THE FOUNDATION

Grasping the Study of Rest and Alertness

At the core of changing your mornings lies a major comprehension of the science behind rest and alertness. Our bodies work on a perplexing framework known as the circadian mood, an inner clock that controls patterns of sharpness and language within a 24-hour time span. This mood is affected by outer prompts, for example, light and obscurity, which signal our bodies when to awaken and when to slow down. Getting a handle on the mechanics of this framework is the most important move toward outfitting its capacity for our potential benefit.

The Job of Circadian Rhythms

Our circadian rhythms accomplish something other than let us know when to rest and when to wake; they assume a vital part in deciding our energy levels, mind-set, and by and large wellbeing. Disturbances to this musicality, for example, those made by unpredictable dozing examples or openness light around evening time, can significantly affect our prosperity. By adjusting our wake-up opportunity to the normal ascent of the sun, we tap into the mood's capability to improve our everyday work. Early morning light openness helps reset our inner clock, advancing a sound rest cycle and working on our readiness during the day.

Melatonin and rest

The chemical melatonin assumes a significant role in our rest-wake cycle. Delivered by the pineal organ in the mind, its levels ascend at night to advance rest and abatement in the first part of the day to work with alertness. Understanding what light openness means for melatonin creation is vital to dominating early rising. By lessening openness to counterfeit light sources around evening time and looking for regular light in the first part of the day, we can urge our bodies to deliver melatonin at the ideal opportunities, supporting the change to turning into a morning person.

Rest Engineering and Quality

Quality rest isn't just about terms; it's additionally about structure. Rest is made up of numerous cycles, each comprising various stages, including REM (fast eye development) and different periods of non-REM rest. These stages are critical for mental capabilities, profound guidelines, and actual wellbeing. A successful morning schedule starts with determining the significance of each rest stage by laying out steady rest and wake times that take into account total and helpful rest cycles.

The Effect of Rest on Wellbeing and Execution

The advantages of adjusting our rest-wake cycle with our circadian rhythms go beyond simple comfort. Research has shown that people who stick to a predictable rest plan will generally have better psychological wellness, higher mental execution, and a decreased risk of persistent diseases. Go-getters frequently report a further developed mindset, more noteworthy efficiency, and an elevated feeling of fulfillment with their lives.

Utilizing Rest Science for Early Rising

Furnished with information on how rest and attentiveness are represented by our inner tickers and impacted by our ways of behaving, we can settle on informed decisions about our morning schedules. Changing our current circumstances to help regular rest designs, overseeing light openness, and regarding the significance of rest engineering are procedures that establish the groundwork for fruitful early rising. By getting it and working with our body's normal rhythms, we can open the way to mornings that are more useful as well as more conducive to our general wellbeing and prosperity.

In summary, the excursion to turning into a go-getter is supported by a profound appreciation for the study of rest and attentiveness. It is through this understanding that we can make a way of life that works on our mornings as well as upgrades our personal satisfaction, no matter how you look at it.

The fantasy of the evening person versus the morning person

The division of evening people and morning people has for some time been a subject of discussion, with society frequently leaning toward the sentimentalism of the go-getter while projecting the evening person as a sorry excuse for uselessness. Nonetheless, this division misrepresents the complicated dance of hereditary qualities, climate, and individual decisions that direct our circadian inclinations. This part intends to expose the fantasies encompassing our intrinsic tendencies towards the evening or morning, introducing a more nuanced comprehension of our ability for change.

Hereditary Inclinations and Adaptability

While hereditary qualities play a part in determining our regular circadian rhythms, suggesting an inclination toward being more ready toward the beginning of the day or night, ongoing examination demonstrates that these propensities are not quite as fixed as once suspected. Our rest and wake cycles are versatile, and with persistence and the right systems, even the most affirmed evening person can move their example to embrace the early morning light. This adaptability highlights the impact of trained instinct and climate over natural inclination, opening the entryway for anybody to turn into an ambitious person, no matter what their hereditary cosmetics.

Social and ecological impacts

The differentiation between evening people and morning people is additionally obscured while thinking about the effects of social and natural elements. The advanced world's consistent network and the predominance of counterfeit lighting have broadened the regular day, pushing our sleep time later and testing our inner clock. This fake augmentation of the day doesn't change our major requirement for supportive rest; it only dislodges it, frequently to our hindrance. By deliberately changing our current circumstances to mirror the regular movement of light and dim, we can direct our bodies back to a more conventional rest-wake cycle.

The Brain Research of Rest Inclinations

Our resting inclinations are not just organic; they are likewise mental. The appeal of the calm evening or the quiet early morning can be as much about the isolation and independence from interruptions these times offer as about any physiological inclination. Perceiving this, we can start to see the decision of when to rise not as a double choice but rather as an inclination that we can move in light of our qualities, objectives, and the requests of our lives.

Moving rest cycles

Changing from an evening person to a prompt riser is certainly not a short-term change; it requires a slow change in rest designs. By steadily moving sleep time and getting up time prior, even by a couple of moments like clockwork, we can permit our body to change without causing unnecessary pressure. This delicate methodology regards our body's regular rhythms while directing them towards our ideal timetable. Close by, adjusting our openness to light, both regular and fake, can help this progress by supporting our body's prompts for rest and alertness.

Embracing a Customized Approach

At last, the excursion from evening person to timely riser is an individual one, reflecting individual needs, ways of life, and obligations. By understanding the flexibility of our resting wake cycles and the variables that impact them, we can create a morning schedule that lines up with our objectives and improves our prosperity. This section isn't a call to neglect the night, but rather a challenge to investigate the advantages of the morning, outfitted with the information that our rest-wake inclinations are an option for us to change.

In dissipating the fantasy of the unchanging evening person and morning person, we open ourselves to the chance of change. There's actually no need to focus on changing what our identity is; it's about advancing how we live to meet our desires. The night might hold its charm; however, the morning offers a new material for those ready to change their rhythms to hold onto it.

Defining Practical Objectives and Assumptions

Leaving on the excursion to turn into a go-getter isn't just about changing your morning timer; it's tied in with rethinking your relationship with the morning and laying out objectives that line up with your vision for a more useful, satisfying life. This section centers around the significance of putting forth reasonable objectives and overseeing assumptions as you progress to getting up on time. It is both practical and compensating to guarantee this change.

The Force of Steady Change

One of the critical techniques for turning into a go-getter is to embrace the force of gradual change. The charm of emotional change can be enticing; however, unexpected changes in other examples can prompt disappointment and difficulties. All things being equal, putting forth an objective to awaken only a couple of moments prior to every day permits your body and mind to continuously change. This approach decreases the shock to your framework, making the change smoother and more likely to stick.

Grasping Your 'Why'

Prior to setting your alert, understanding your motivations is pivotal. Might it be said that you are hoping to carve out a calm opportunity for yourself, improve your efficiency, or maybe partake in the quietness of the morning? Explaining your 'why' gives guidance and motivation, energizing your responsibility in any event when the compulsion to hit nap serious areas of strength for is. Objectives established in private qualities and yearnings are definitely more convincing than those in view of outside assumptions or cultural standards.

Making brilliant objectives

To guarantee your initial rising objectives are attainable, they ought to be explicit, quantifiable, feasible, persistent, and time-bound (Savvy). Rather than an obscure desire to "get up ahead of schedule," a Savvy objective would be, "For the following month, I will get up at 6:30 AM, 15 minutes sooner than my ongoing wake-up time, to contemplate for 10 minutes prior to beginning my day." This clarity changes the goal right into it, giving a substantial structure to progress.

Overseeing Assumptions

Progressing as a go-getter is a cycle loaded with victories and mishaps. It's essential to deal with your assumptions, understanding that a few mornings will be simpler than others. Embracing adaptability and excusing yourself for infrequent slips can assist with keeping up with inspiration. Keep in mind that the objective is progress, not flawlessness. Celebrating little triumphs enroute builds up a sure way of behaving and keeps you on target toward your bigger goal.

Changing objectives on a case-by-case basis

As you progress in your excursion, you might find that your underlying objectives need change. Maybe getting up considerably earlier becomes attractive, or you find new morning exercises that enhance your everyday practice. Consistently reconsidering and changing your objectives guarantees they stay in line with your developing needs and way of life. This unique methodology permits you to persistently refine your morning schedule, guaranteeing it generally serves your most elevated needs.

In defining practical objectives and assumptions, we make a guide for change that recognizes our ongoing propensities, regards our speed of progress, and praises our more profound inspirations. This insightful planning lays the foundation for a fruitful change to an early-rising, transforming goal into a reachable, life-improving reality. With every morning we welcome the day a piece prior, we step closer to the individual we try to be, completely embracing the commitment and potential that the early hours offer.

Creating Your Optimal Morning Schedule

The change to turning into a go-getter isn't just about the demonstration of getting up ahead of schedule; it's about how you manage the time that follows. Creating your ideal morning schedule is a fundamental stage in this excursion, transforming those additional hours into a safe haven for self-awareness, efficiency, and prosperity. This section guides you through planning a morning schedule that reverberates with your objectives, stimulates your day, and changes your life.

Distinguishing key exercises

The most vital phase in creating your ideal morning schedule is recognizing exercises that line up with your objectives and give you pleasure. Whether it's contemplation, working out, perusing, journaling, or basically partaking in a tranquil mug of espresso, these exercises ought to stimulate and move you. There's really no need to focus on filling consistently with undertakings; instead, pick activities that set an uplifting vibe for the day ahead. Ponder what exercises leave you feeling satisfied and integrate them into your mornings.

Grouping and timing

Whenever you've recognized your key exercises, think about their arrangement and timing. A few exercises, similar to exercise or contemplation, could act as strong starters, indicating to your body and psyche that the day has started. Others, such as arranging your day or perusing, could fit better once you're completely alert. Explore different avenues regarding the request for exercises to find what best suits your regular mood and improves your morning experience.

Making a custom

Changing your morning exercises into a custom can fundamentally influence your eagerness for an early ascent. A custom, in contrast to an everyday practice, conveys a feeling of holiness and purposefulness. It's what you do, yet the way that you make it happen—moving toward your exercises with care and appreciation. This outlook shift can transform unremarkable undertakings into snapshots of happiness and reflection, making your morning schedule something you anticipate every day.

Adaptability inside construction

While having an organized routine is valuable, it's similarly critical to take into consideration adaptability. A few mornings could require changes, whether because of unforeseen requests, changes in your mindset, or just the longing to take a stab at a new thing. Permitting yourself the beauty to adjust your daily practice depending on the situation guarantees that it stays strong as opposed to prohibitive. Keep in mind that the objective of your morning schedule is to upgrade your prosperity, not to turn into one more wellspring of stress.

Reflection and change

At last, standard reflection on your morning schedule is vital for its drawn-out progress. Carve out the opportunity to evaluate what's working and what isn't. Are there exercises that never again serve you? Is it true that you are reliably skirting a piece of your daily schedule, and provided that this is true, why? This continuous assessment guarantees that your morning schedule develops with you, staying in line with your ongoing objectives and necessities.

Creating your ideal morning schedule is a profoundly private cycle, one that offers significant compensation for those ready to contribute the time and effort. By insightfully choosing exercises, making a custom around them, and taking into consideration adaptability, you set up for mornings that start your day as well as really enhance your life. As you tweak your daily practice, you'll find that rising early isn't just about the additional time—it's tied in with changing those hours into an establishment for a more deliberate, happy life.

Embracing the Test and Observing Advancement

The journey to becoming a morning person is loaded with difficulties, yet it is likewise ready with open doors for development and self-disclosure. This last mark of the section centers around embracing the inescapable impediments you will confront and the significance of commending your advancement, regardless of how little. These snapshots of acknowledgment are urgent for keeping up with inspiration and supporting the positive changes you're making in your life.

Expecting Difficulties

The way to work on any propensity, particularly your wake-up time, is rarely smooth. Expecting provokes, for example, the compulsion to hit rest, sensations of drowsiness, or days when inspiration melts away. Recognize these obstructions not as disappointments but rather as indispensable pieces of the excursion. By expecting them, you can plan systems ahead of time, whether it's putting your morning timer across the room, laying out a convincing motivation to get up right away, or making a morning playlist to invigorate your everyday practice.

Systems for Beating Obstacles

At the point when you experience difficulties, having a toolbox of systems becomes priceless. This could incorporate helping yourself to remember your 'why,' zeroing in on the advantages you've previously seen, or changing your current circumstances to all the more likely help your objectives. For instance, assuming you find it hard to awaken when it's dim, consider a dawn-morning timer that mimics regular sunlight. In the event that inspiration is your obstacle, plan your mornings around an action you truly appreciate. These methodologies are not tied to keeping away from obstructions but rather about exploring through them with versatility and adaptability.

The Significance of Self-Sympathy

Self-sympathy is an indispensable part of this excursion. There will be mornings when, notwithstanding your earnest attempts, you neglect to ascend at your planned time. Rather than unforgiving self-analysis, offer yourself generosity and understanding. Ponder what turned out badly and how you can change, yet do as such with the same sympathy you would stretch out to a companion. This caring methodology energizes a positive mentality, making it more straightforward to refocus.

Observing Your Advancement

Each day you get up earlier than you used to is a triumph worth celebrating. Perceive and praise your advancement, as far as getting up ahead of schedule as well as the way it influences your life. Maybe you're more useful, set aside greater opportunity for leisure activities, or feel improved intellectually and truly. Commending these successes, enormous or small, supports your responsibility and helps you remember the substantial advantages of your endeavors.

Thinking about Your Excursion

Intermittently consider your excursion from where you began to where you are presently. This reflection isn't just about recognizing the advancement in getting up ahead of schedule, but additionally understanding what this change has meant for different parts of your life. What examples have you realized? How has your view of mornings changed? This reflection offers important experiences that can motivate future objectives and further self-awareness.

Embracing the test of turning into a morning person and commending each forward-moving step is about more than working on a propensity; it is about embracing a way of life that cultivates development, efficiency, and prosperity. As you progress forward this way, let your difficulties be your educators and your advancement a wellspring of pride. This excursion is interestingly yours, and every morning is another chance to carry on with your existence with goal and delight.

CHAPTER 2: CRAFTING YOUR 5 AM BLUEPRINT

Grasping Your Body's Normal Rhythms

To set out on the excursion of ascending at 5 AM, it is, in any case, crucial to have a profound comprehension of your body's regular rhythms. Our bodies are administered by circadian rhythms, inward clocks that direct our rest and wake cycles, chemical delivery, and other essential physiological cycles. These rhythms are affected by natural signs and are generally quite light, which assists with managing our feeling of constant Embracing early mornings begins with adjusting your craving to get up at 5 AM with these inborn rhythms, guaranteeing that your body can adjust without trouble.

Distinguishing Your Ongoing Rhythms

The most vital phase in this arrangement is to distinguish your ongoing rest designs. This includes noticing your regular rest propensities for more than seven days without the impedance of cautions. Note the times you normally nod off and awaken. This exercise gives a pattern comprehension of your body's ongoing musicality, offering bits of knowledge into how much change is expected to accomplish your 5 AM objective.

The Job of Light

Light plays a vital role in changing your circadian mood. Openness to normal light in the first part of the day flags your body to awaken, while darkening lights at night advance a feeling of lethargy. Utilizing light can assist with resetting your inner clock to help with a previous wake-up time. Consolidating morning light openness, either by venturing outside or utilizing a light treatment box, can essentially help with moving your wake time prior in a characteristic and supportable way.

Slow Changes

Unexpected changes to your rest schedule can bump into your framework, prompting expanded exhaustion and diminishing, generally speaking, rest quality. All things considered, progressive changes are critical. Fire by awakening only 15 minutes sooner than expected, step by step moving your get-up time prior until you arrive at the 5 AM mark. This progressive shift permits your body to adjust without critical shock, making the change smoother and more manageable.

Paying attention to your body

As you make these changes, it's pivotal to pay attention to your body's signs. In the event that you're feeling unreasonably drained or battling to nod off at a prior time, it very well might be an indication to dial back the progress pace. It's likewise vital to guarantee you're getting sufficient rest generally; getting up at 5 AM shouldn't essentially cut into your complete rest time. Change your sleep time likewise to maintain a solid rest period.

The Significance of Consistency

At last, consistency in your rest and wake times supports your body's new mood. Attempt to keep your wake-up time reliable across the week, including the ends of the week. While it very well may be enticing to work on days off, keeping a predictable wake-up time fortifies your body's inner clock, making getting up at 5 AM a characteristic piece of your everyday cadence.

Understanding and regarding your body's normal rhythms is the establishment whereupon the 5 AM upset is fabricated. By adjusting your initial rising objective to these rhythms, you set up for an effective progress to awakening stimulated and prepared to live every moment to the fullest, consistently.

Setting up the prior night

The key to an effective 5 a.m. awakening starts the prior night. Planning is critical to guaranteeing you awaken on time as well as making the early hours of your day as useful and pleasant as could really be expected. This segment of the part dives into the nighttime schedules and propensities that make you ready for a smooth morning, putting you in a good position before your head even raises a ruckus around town.

The Force of a Night Schedule

Laying out a quiet evening schedule signals to your body that now is the ideal time to slow down and get ready for rest. This routine can incorporate exercises that advance unwinding and assist with bringing down your pulse, setting up your body and brain for rest. Consider integrating perusing, delicate extending, contemplation, or a steaming shower into your evening schedule. These exercises help you nod off more effectively as well as improve the nature of your rest, guaranteeing that you awaken revived and prepared to embrace the day.

Innovation Detox

Quite possibly the most significant change you can make to your nighttime schedule is executing an innovation detox. The blue light discharged by screens can slow down your body's development of melatonin, the chemical responsible for controlling rest. By setting a hard stop on screen time, something like one hour before bed, you permit your psyche to loosen up and your body to plan for rest normally. This detox period can be supplanted with any of your chosen loosening exercises, further improving your pre-rest schedule.

Planning for the first part of the day

A smooth morning begins with disposing of potential snags that could disturb your promising beginning. Spread out all that you'll require for the morning the prior night. This could incorporate your exercise garments, a prepared breakfast, or a plan for the day in the afternoon. By eliminating the need to decide or look for things in the first part of the day, you limit grinding and make it more straightforward to kick off your three-day weekend just subsequent to awakening.

The significance of a climate that welcomes rest

Establishing a climate helpful for rest is essential for guaranteeing that you awaken feeling rested. This includes something other than an agreeable sleeping pad and cushions; think about the temperature, commotion, and light in your room. A cooler room temperature, ordinarily between 60 and 67°F (15 and 19°C), has been displayed to work with better rest. Utilizing power outage draperies to kill light and background noise to muffle problematic sounds can likewise essentially further develop rest quality.

An Evening of Value Rest

At long last, the foundation of getting up at 5 AM feeling invigorated is an evening of value rest. This implies focusing on the amount of your rest as well as its quality. Following a predictable sleep schedule, guaranteeing your room is a safe haven for rest, and taking part in loosening up exercises before bed all contribute to a profound, helpful night's rest. By making these arrangements a part of your daily practice, you set yourself up for a fruitful early morning rise, completely energized and prepared to handle the day with energy and excitement.

The groundwork for a 5 a.m. awakening begins well before the morning timer sounds. It's the smart schedules and decisions made the night prior to that that encourage you to rise early and take full advantage of your morning hours. With these procedures set up, you'll see that getting up at 5 AM turns out to be, to a lesser extent, a test and even more of a remunerating start to your day.

Establishing a Rest-Instigating Climate

Establishing a climate that is helpful for rest is as basic to your 5 a.m. insurgency as the discipline for an early ascent. This climate upholds nodding off rapidly as well as guarantees that the rest you get is profound and supportive, preparing you for the day ahead. The ideal rest climate tends to have a few key elements: light, sound, temperature, and solace, each custom-fitted to upgrade your body's regular rest instruments.

The Job of Dimness in Rest Quality

Light openness assumes a huge part in flagging your mind about the hour of day, influencing your circadian rhythms and melatonin creation. To develop a rest-prompting climate, limiting light contamination in your bedroom is fundamental. Power outage draperies or eye covers can be viable devices for shutting out any outside light sources, including streetlamps or early-day break lights, guaranteeing your rest climate stays dim and helpful for ceaseless rest.

Overseeing Sound for a Quiet Rest

Commotion can fundamentally upset rest, keeping you from nodding off or waking you during the evening. Establishing a sound climate that advances continuous rest could include utilizing background noise or applications that muffle foundation clamor with relieving, predictable sounds. On the other hand, earplugs can be a basic yet successful answer for those in especially uproarious conditions, assisting with maintaining a calm rest space.

Advancing Room Temperature

Temperature significantly affects rest quality. A room that is too hot or too cold can intrude on your rest cycle, making it hard to nod off or stay unconscious. The ideal temperature for rest is around 60–67°F (15–19°C), as cooler temperatures support the regular dunk in your body's center temperature that happens during rest. Changing your indoor regulator or utilizing breathable, dampness-wicking bedding can assist with keeping up with this ideal resting climate.

Guaranteeing Solace and Backing

Your bedding, pad, and bedding assume an immediate part in your rest quality. Putting resources into agreeable, steady bedding and cushions that line up with your dozing position can have a huge effect on your rest quality and, likewise, your capacity to get up at 5 AM feeling rested. Likewise, picking bedding that suits your comfort inclination and the season can assist with keeping you at the right temperature over the course of the evening.

A Safe- Haven for Rest

Your room ought to be a safe haven for rest, liberated from interruptions, and helpful for unwinding. This implies eliminating work materials, hardware, and different wellsprings of stress or excitement from your rest climate. Making a space dedicated exclusively to rest can improve your psychological relationship between your room and rest, making it simpler to slow down around evening time and wake up revived in the first part of the day.

Creating a rest-prompting climate is a basic move toward your excursion toward turning into a go-getter. By focusing on the subtleties of your rest space, you can fundamentally work on the nature of your rest, making getting up at 5 a.m. plausible as well as a delight. This climate makes way for soothing evenings that fuel enthusiastic mornings, permitting you to open your maximum capacity each morning in turn.

Embracing the Psychological Shift

The progress toward getting up at 5 AM isn't exclusively about changing your actual propensities; it's similarly about embracing a psychological shift. This change includes changing how you see mornings, the worth you assign to your most memorable hours, and the attitude with which you approach every day. It's a complete reconsideration of your relationship with time and an affirmation of the significant effect that early rising can have on your life.

Rethinking Your Morning's Motivation

The most vital phase of this psychological shift is rethinking the reason for your mornings. Rather than survey the early hours as only a chance to plan for work or different commitments, consider them to be a chance for self-improvement and taking care of oneself. This time can be dedicated to exercises that you might struggle to squeeze into the remainder of your day, like activity, reflection, perusing, or arranging. By reconsidering your mornings as holy time for yourself, you normally start to value getting up ahead of schedule as a vital aspect of opening up this potential.

Defeating mental obstructions

Large numbers of us harbor subliminal convictions that make getting up early appear to be unconquerable. These can incorporate profoundly instilled thoughts that we are not morning individuals or that rest is more important than the tranquil isolation of the early hours. Conquering these psychological boundaries requires a cognizant effort to challenge and reevaluate negative contemplations. Perceive that these convictions are propensities for thought instead of fixed insights about your character. With training and persistence, you can shift your mentality to one that embraces the potential outcomes of the early morning.

Representation and Assertions

Representation and confirmations are amazing assets in affecting this psychological shift. Invest time each night imagining your ideal morning, seeing yourself awakening with energy, and anticipating the harmony and efficiency that look for you. Match this perception with positive confirmations about your capacity to rise early and take full advantage of your mornings. These practices support your obligation to the 5 a.m. unrest and reinforce your faith in your ability to change.

Setting Reasonable Assumptions

A piece of the psychological shift includes setting practical assumptions for your initial mornings. Understand that only one out of every odd morning will be completely useful or joyfully peaceful. Occasionally, you could battle to get up, or life's eccentricity might disturb your arranged schedules. Tolerating these variances with elegance and adaptability is urgent. It's not the immaculate execution of your morning schedule that characterizes achievement; rather, you proceeded with an obligation to the interaction and your ability to adjust.

Developing Appreciation and Reflection

At long last, embracing the psychological shift implies developing a feeling of appreciation and reflection. Utilize your initial mornings to ponder what you're thankful for and the progress you're making towards your own objectives. This training not only begins your day optimistically, but in addition, it supports the worth of the time you've asserted for yourself. It changes early, ascending from a test into a loved open door, energizing your inspiration, and extending your obligation to the 5 AM transformation.

Embracing the psychological shift is an urgent part of opening your mind each morning in turn. It's about more than changing when you awaken; it's tied in with changing why you awaken and how you approach your day. With this psychological shift, the early morning turns into a material for self-awareness, efficiency, and harmony, essentially modifying your life's direction.

CHAPTER 3: THE 5 AM PRODUCTIVITY BOOST

Amplifying Calm Hours for Concentration and Inventiveness

The quietness of the early morning, when our general surroundings rests, holds an undiscovered repository of efficiency and imagination. In these tranquil hours, liberated from the interferences and requests that fill the remainder of our day, our psyches can meander, investigate, and jump profoundly into the domains of concentration and imagination that are much of the time inaccessible during the buzzing about of sunlight hours.

The Study of Quiet

Research recommends that quiet, in its most perfect structure, can recover synapses and cultivate new degrees of reasoning. In the early morning, the shortfall of clamor contamination, both physical and computerized, establishes a special climate for our minds. This peacefulness permits us to enter a state of stream all the more effectively, where our work or imaginative undertakings can continue without the obstructions that interruptions erect.

Outfitting the Force of the Pre-Day Break Psyche

Some time before sunrise, our brains are more equipped for direct and consistent reasoning. It is during these hours that we can bridle this lucidity for errands requiring profound concentration, like composition, coding, or arranging complex tasks. The pre-first light brain, cleaned up continuously concerns and interruptions, is prepared for leaps forward and bits of knowledge.

Methodologies for Utilizing Calm Time

To take advantage of these calm hours, it's fundamental to start with a goal. Conclude the night prior to what assignment or project will be your concentration. This precautionary navigation guarantees you can jump straight into profound work without the loss of motion of decision that frequently goes with the beginning of a day.

Making a dedicated space for your initial morning work is likewise pivotal. This space ought to be liberated from mess and intended to motivate concentration and inventiveness. Whether it's a work space, a kitchen table, or a comfortable corner with a work area, this actual space signals to your mind that now is the right time to take part in profound work.

Embracing the Cadence of the Early Hours

The cadence of the early morning, set apart by the progressive easing up of the sky and the world's sluggish arousal, can be a strong partner in your efficiency process. Adjusting your work to these normal prompts gives a feeling of congruity and progress, improving your capacity to focus and make decisions.

The Prize for Early Morning Efficiency

The most unmistakable prize of augmenting the peaceful hours of the early morning comes as progress on your most significant activities. This advancement, accomplished before the day formally starts, gives a significant feeling of achievement and force. A force conveys you forward, causing the other day's undertakings to feel more reasonable and reachable.

All in all, the early morning hours offer a safe-haven for those trying to upgrade their efficiency and imagination. By embracing the quietness and isolation of the pre-first light, you can open degrees of concentration and development that set the vibe for a satisfying and effective day. This is the substance of the 5 AM efficiency support — a clear-cut advantage in the weapons store of the best people.

Focusing on undertakings and setting goals

The peaceful quietude of the early morning is something other than a background for efficiency; it's a material whereupon we can paint our expectations for the afternoon. Focusing on errands and setting clear expectations during these early hours isn't simply a practice in association — an essential move adjusts our energies to our most basic goals, guaranteeing that we channel our endeavors where they are generally required and effective.

The Specialty of Prioritization

In the tranquility of sunrise, with a brain revived from rest and unburdened by constant interruptions, we are in an ideal state to assess our undertakings with clarity and wisdom. This is the second time we ask ourselves: What are the key results I wish to accomplish today? Which errands, whenever finished, could have the greatest effect on my objectives? Prioritization in the early morning is tied in with distinguishing these high-influence exercises and focusing on them before the world awakens and requests our consideration somewhere else.

Setting Clear Expectations

Setting goals remains closely connected with focusing on assignments. It's tied in with characterizing the 'why' behind the 'what.' When we set expectations, we're not simply posting errands; we're associating them with our bigger objectives and values. This association diverts each errand from a simple thing on a plan for the day into a significant stage towards a more prominent goal. Whether it's advancing on an undertaking, upgrading individual prosperity, or extending connections, every goal set in the serenity of the early morning fills in as a directing star for the day's excursion.

Focusing on Undertakings and Setting Expectations

At the break of first light, when the world is still and our psyches are clear, lies the ideal chance to make plans to arrive at our day. This second, immaculate by the messiness and bedlam that sunlight hours bring, is great for focusing on assignments and setting aims. It's a training of arranging, however of adjusting our everyday activities to our more extensive life objectives, guaranteeing that every day is a step in the right direction in our excursion.

The Groundwork of Concentration

Prioritization starts with reflection. In the calm of the early morning, we have the psychological space to consider what is really significant. This is an ideal opportunity to ask ourselves: What must I achieve today to feel effective by the end of the day? What will draw me nearer to my objectives? This reflection assists us with filtering through the heap assignments competing for our focus, it are genuinely basic to distinguish those not many that.

Making a Guide for the Afternoon

With our needs distinguished, we then, at that point, set our aims for the afternoon. This is more than simply posting assignments; it includes imagining the results we want and the means necessary to accomplish them. Setting expectations is tied in with pervading our undertakings with reason, changing them from simple things on an agenda into responsibilities lined up with our own and proficient goals.

The Job of Deliberateness

Deliberateness carries a layer of profundity to our initial daytime arrangements. It's about what we really want to do as well as why it makes a difference. This understanding fills our inspiration and guides our concentration, guaranteeing that we contribute our energies carefully. By setting expectations, we focus on the actual undertakings as well as the qualities and objectives they address.

Embracing Adaptability

While focusing on assignments and setting goals, embracing flexibility is vital. The day ahead may bring surprising moves or open doors that require adjustments to our arrangements. The key is to stay centered around our all-encompassing goals, adjusting our needs on a case-by-case basis while remaining consistent with the goals we've set for ourselves.

The far-reaching influence of morning priority

The demonstration of focusing on undertakings and setting goals toward the beginning of the day has a far-reaching influence, impacting the hours that follow as well as our more extensive sense of direction and progress. Today, custom guarantees that every day isn't simply one more range of time yet a significant stage toward understanding our most profound yearnings. It's training that upgrades our efficiency as well as improves our lives, making every morning the foundation of a reason-driven life.

Defeating Lingering and Gathering Speed

As the sunrise deadheads across the sky, painting the world with the main light of day, the individuals who ascend at 5 AM stand at an interesting intersection. Here, in the calm before the noise of day-to-day existence starts, lies a once-in-a lifetime chance to design, but not to act. This early morning second is the ideal remedy to dawdling, offering a new record whereupon to gather speed for the day ahead.

The Prompt riser's Procedure Against Stalling

Tarrying, the cheat of time, frequently strikes, assuming some pretense of overpowering undertakings or the appeal of later. However, in the early morning, with the day's maximum capacity spread out before us, we find a clarity and reason that can slice through wavering. The way to utilize these early hours is to begin small. By choosing an underlying undertaking that is both significant and reasonable, we connect with our feeling of achievement from the beginning, establishing an uplifting vibe that can bring us joy as the day progresses.

Gathering Speed with Each Assignment

Force, once started, has an intensifying impact. Each undertaking finished, regardless of how little, energizes our certainty and inspiration, moving us forward. This early morning force is likened to a snowball moving down a slope, building up size and momentum with each turn. Making a chain response of efficiency begins with that first, conscious move made at the beginning of the day.

The Mental Lift of Early Wins

There's a mental elevate that comes from ticking off undertakings in the early hours, when the world has yet to set its expectations for us. These early wins are not simply things marked off a rundown; they are certifications of our capacity to assume command over our day and to coordinate our way as opposed to being driven by it. This feeling of control is a strong inspiration, building up our purpose to handle additional difficult errands as the day advances.

Utilizing the Morning to Handle the Most Overwhelming Errands

The insight of the 5 a.m. start lies not simply in the hours it adds to our day, but in the way it empowers us to move toward our most overwhelming undertakings. With our energy at its pinnacle and interruptions at their nadir, we are in the most ideal state to face the assignments we could somehow or another stay away from. It is here, in the peaceful assurance of the early morning, that we can break the pattern of delaying, transforming our most imposing difficulties into accomplishments.

The Groundbreaking Force of the 5 AM Start

Embracing the 5 AM start isn't simply about getting up ahead of schedule; it's tied in with arousing to our maximum capacity. By utilizing these first, valuable hours to conquer delaying and gather speed, we unlock an extraordinary power that stretches out a long way past the bounds of the morning. Training develops discipline, cultivates efficiency, and ingrains a feeling of achievement that enlightens the remainder of our day. In the calm of the early morning, we discover a genuine sense of harmony of another first light yet the commitment of a more useful, deliberate life.

Developing care and deliberateness

In predawn tranquility, when the world is a murmur and the day extends ahead immaculately, there's a significant chance to develop a more profound sense of care and deliberateness. For the people who embrace the 5 AM upset, this peaceful time isn't just an opportunity to get an early advantage on the day's undertakings; it is also a hallowed space for establishing oneself in the present, establishing the vibe for the hours to come.

Embracing the Quiet for Careful Reflection

The quiet of the early morning is material for reflection, a chance to interface with our internal identities before the requests of the day grab hold. This is the second time to participate in exercises that encourage care, like contemplation, journaling, or just sitting in calm reflection. Thusly, we develop a condition of quiet mindfulness that illuminates our expectations and activities over the course of the day, guaranteeing they are lined up with our basic beliefs and long-term objectives.

Setting Expectations with Clearness and Reason

The demonstration of setting expectations is raised in the early morning, liberated from interruptions and the impact of outer tensions. It's a chance to obviously characterize what we wish to accomplish and why, mixing our objectives with a feeling of direction that reverberates on a more profound level. This clarity of aim goes about as a compass, directing our choices and activities with a center that is both careful and purposeful.

The Force of Perception

Perception is a powerful device in the early hours, permitting us to imagine the day ahead not simply as far as what we need to do, yet the way in which we need to be. Envisioning ourselves exploring the day with beauty, productivity, and versatility sows the seeds for these characteristics to thrive. Through representation, we set up our psyche and soul for the difficulties and valuable open doors that lie ahead, supporting our ability to meet them with a positive and proactive disposition.

Incorporating care into day-to-day schedules

The care developed in the early morning doesn't end as the sun rises; it's woven into the texture of our day. Each errand, collaboration, and choice is drawn closer with an uplifted feeling of presence and purposefulness. This careful methodology changes routine exercises into demonstrations of contemplation, transforming the unremarkable into snapshots of happiness and revelation. It's training that improves our efficiency as well as enhances our lives, consistently leading to development and satisfaction.

The Groundbreaking Effect of Early Morning Care

The choice to ascend at 5 AM and participate in rehearsals that upgrade care and deliberateness is extraordinary. It's a pledge to live all the more gainfully, however more definitively. This early wake-up routine turns into the foundation of a way of life that values presence, reason, and self-awareness. As the days unfurl, the advantages of this training increase, affecting each part of our lives and leaving an enduring effect on our prosperity and our general surroundings. Through the calm discipline of the early hours, we find the force of a second as well as the capability that could only be described as epic.

CHAPTER 4: ENHANCING YOUR WELL-BEING AT 5 AM

Actual Wellness: A 5 AM Custom

Rundown: This part stresses the significance of integrating actual activity into the early morning schedule. It examines how participating in actual work at 5 AM can support energy levels, upgrade temperament, and set an uplifting vibe for the afternoon. It recommends different types of activity appropriate for the early hours, underscoring the flexibility of this training to individual wellness levels and inclinations.

Healthful Starting point for an Empowered Day

Rundown: Spotlights on the meaning of a careful and nutritious breakfast following an early ascent. It investigates how the principal feast of the day can be streamlined to fuel the body and mind, offering reasonable tips on planning speedy, sound, and invigorating breakfast choices that line up with a 5 AM start.

Mental and Profound Equilibrium Through Morning Practices

Rundown: Features the advantages of early morning practices like reflection, journaling, or yoga for mental and close to home prosperity. This part dives into how committing time to these exercises at 5 AM can upgrade mental lucidity, lessen pressure, and develop a positive outlook for the day ahead.

The Job of Morning Daylight in Controlling Circadian Rhythms

Synopsis: Analyzes the effect of regular light openness in the early morning on rest examples and by and large well-being. It talks about the science behind circadian rhythms and how morning daylight can assist with managing these organic cycles, prompting further developed rest quality and energy levels.

Making a Morning Schedule Customized to Individual Prosperity

Synopsis: Urges perusers to plan a customized 5 AM standard that takes special care of their novel prosperity needs. This part gives direction on the most proficient method to evaluate individual wellbeing and wellbeing objectives and incorporate practices into the morning that help physical, mental, and close to home wellbeing, cultivating an all encompassing way to deal with prosperity from the outset of the day.

Wholesome Starting point for an Empowered Day

As the world blends and the main light of sunrise breaks our skyline, the decisions in the calm of the early morning can make way for a stimulated and useful day. Among these decisions, maybe none is more basic than how we break our daily quick. The demonstration of feeding our bodies first thing isn't simply a custom of food yet a statement of aim for the day ahead.

The Force of a Careful Breakfast

In the tranquility of the early hours, finding opportunity to plan and partake in a nutritious breakfast is a demonstration of taking care of oneself that delivers profits over the course of the day. It's a second to be available, to relish the flavors and surfaces of our food, and to pay attention to our body's requirements. This careful way to deal with our most memorable feast urges us to pursue decisions that are flavorful as well as profoundly sustaining.

Energizing Body and Mind

The science is clear: the food varieties we devour at breakfast can altogether affect our energy levels, mental capability, and profound prosperity. A dinner wealthy in entire grains, lean proteins, sound fats, and new natural products or vegetables gives a consistent arrival of energy, keeping us filled and centered. About making an establishment upholds actual perseverance as well as smartness too.

Fast, Solid, Invigorating Choices

With regards to a 5 AM start, straightforwardness and speed are vital. However, fast doesn't need to mean compromised quality. Short-term oats absorbed almond milk, finished off with nuts and berries; a smoothie loaded with spinach, banana, and protein powder; or an omelet stacked with vegetables and a side of entire grain toast can be generally ready with insignificant fight. These choices guarantee that even the most time-squeezed among us can begin the day with a dinner that is both fast and gainful.

Lining up with Individual Wellbeing Objectives

Our morning dinner is likewise a chance to adjust our everyday practices to more extensive wellbeing and health objectives. Whether it's consolidating more plant-based food varieties, overseeing glucose levels, or supporting admission of specific supplements, the decisions at breakfast can serve these finishes. It's tied in with customizing our way to deal with sustenance, perceiving that there's nobody size-fits-all arrangement.

An Impetus for a Better Way of life

Embracing the discipline of a nutritious breakfast at 5 AM accomplishes something other than launch our digestion; it establishes a vibe of care and deliberateness that can impact our decisions over the course of the day. It's an initial phase in an excursion towards a better, more cognizant approach to everyday life. As we relish our morning dinner in the calm before the day unfurls, we accomplish something beyond feed our bodies. We support our spirits, fuel our desires, and confirm our obligation to a day to day existence lived with reason and health.

Mental and Profound Equilibrium Through Morning Practices

As sunrise's delicate light saturates the tranquility of the early morning, people leaving on the 5 AM venture have an interesting an open door to develop actual strength, yet mental and close to home flexibility too. In these tranquil hours, the world offers a safe-haven for rehearses that cultivate internal harmony and profound balance, starting a trend for the day ahead.

Embracing Isolation for Mental Lucidity

The isolation of the early morning is an uncommon ware in our quick moving, consistently associated lives. It's when interruptions are at their most minimal, taking into consideration an unmatched spotlight on mental and profound practices. Reflection, with its bunch structures, turns into a foundation of today custom. Whether it's care contemplation, centered around the breath and the current second, or directed perceptions driving us through tranquil scenes of the brain, these practices clear the psychological mess, lessen pressure, and improve our close to home deftness.

Journaling: A Way to Self-Disclosure

Close by reflection, journaling remains as an amazing asset for profound prosperity. The demonstration of putting pen to paper in the early morning accomplishes more than catch considerations; it's a course of self-reflection and disclosure. Through journaling, we can define objectives, offer thanks, or just empty the concerns that burden our consciences. This training fills in as both a mirror and a guide, mirroring our deepest contemplations and feelings while directing us towards self-awareness and understanding.

Yoga: Joining Body and Psyche

Yoga, in the serenity of the early hours, turns into a dance of breath and development, an actual reflection that fortifies the body while quieting the brain. As we travel through the stances, we're welcome to be completely present, to draw in with every breath, and to notice the sensations inside our bodies. This actual practice offers a significant effect on our psychological and close to home states, lessening uneasiness and cultivating a feeling of internal quiet that we convey with us over the course of the day.

Developing a Positive Mentality

These morning rehearses on the whole add to a positive mentality, a focal point through which we can see the difficulties and chances of the day with good faith and versatility. The psychological and close to home equilibrium we develop at 5 AM doesn't simply disseminate as the day advances; it turns into a piece of us, impacting our collaborations, our choices, and our insights.

An Establishment for Profound Prosperity

The obligation to mental and close to home practices at 5 AM establishes a groundwork for profound prosperity that is both profound and strong. It's an everyday reaffirmation of our devotion to taking care of oneself, to understanding and dealing with our feelings, and to exploring the intricacies of existence with elegance and dexterity. As we embrace these practices in the tranquility of the morning, we're not simply getting ready for the day ahead; we're putting resources into a long period of profound wellbeing and equilibrium.

The Job of Morning Daylight in Controlling Circadian Rhythms

In the quiet of early day break, as the world enlightens with the primary light of day, there lies a significant chance to adjust our interior clock to the regular world. This arrangement, basic for our physical and psychological well-being, relies on our openness to the morning daylight, a characteristic prompt that directs our circadian rhythms.

Concordance with the Normal World

Our bodies are intended to match up with the pattern of constantly, a musicality directed by the regular habitat. However, in our advanced lives, loaded up with fake light and screen time, this association frequently becomes disturbed. The act of hello the dawn, of venturing into the crisp morning air to luxuriate in the early light, is a demonstration of reconnection. It's an indication of the world past our screens and timetables, a world represented by the rising and setting of the sun.

Improving Rest and Energy Levels

Openness to morning daylight assumes a critical part in setting our inner clock, motioning toward our bodies when now is the ideal time to wake and when now is the ideal time to rest. This regular guideline of our rest wake cycle is essential for profound, supportive rest, which thus influences our energy levels, state of mind, and generally wellbeing. By embracing the morning light, we wake all the more normally as well as lay the preparation for better rest around evening time, making an upright pattern of rest and action.

Helping Temperament and Prosperity

Past its effect on rest, the morning light conveys benefits for our psychological and close to home prosperity. Daylight sets off the arrival of serotonin, a synapse related with a lift in mind-set and a sensation of quiet and concentration. This early portion of normal light can assist with combatting sensations of gloom and tension, offering a delicate, regular method for elevating our spirits as we start our day.

An Impetus for a Better Way of life

Coordinating morning daylight into our routine energizes something beyond a change in our rest cycle; it welcomes a more extensive hug of a better way of life. This straightforward demonstration can be an impetus for other invigorating practices, for example, morning activity or contemplation, further improving our prosperity. It's a stage towards living together as one with our body's regular rhythms and the climate, cultivating a feeling of equilibrium and wellbeing.

Customizing the Experience

The quest for morning light is certainly not a one-size-fits-all undertaking. Contingent upon our geological area, the season, and our own timetable, the manner in which we coordinate this training into our lives might change. Whether it's a concise walk, partaking in some espresso on the gallery, or just opening the shades to let the light occupy the room, what makes a difference is the cognizant work to associate with the normal musicality of the day. This purposeful act of looking for morning daylight upgrades our physical and emotional wellness as well as develops our relationship with the normal world, establishing us right now and helping us to remember the straightforward, significant excellence of day break's initial light.

Sustaining Connections in the Calm of Day break

In the quiet hours of the early morning, there lies a remarkable open door for self-awareness as well as for extending the bonds we share with those nearest to us. While the world actually rests, the 5 AM hour offers a quiet setting for sustaining connections, when interruptions are insignificant and the psyche is clear, taking into consideration significant associations with prosper.

Making Shared Minutes

The demonstration of imparting the early morning to an accomplice, relative, or companion can change a customary daily schedule into a loved custom. Whether it's setting up a tranquil breakfast together, sharing objectives and desires for the day ahead, or essentially partaking in some tea peacefully, these minutes become a safe-haven of association. In the quiet of sunrise, discussions stream all the more uninhibitedly, considering a more profound trade of contemplations, sentiments, and backing.

Building a Groundwork of Help

These common early hours encourage a feeling of cooperation and shared help. Setting and examining everyday goals or difficulties gives lucidity to the day ahead as well as lays out a groundwork of understanding and sympathy inside the relationship. Realizing you have somebody who shares your objectives and difficulties can be a strong wellspring of inspiration and support.

The Advantage of Full focus

In the present speedy world, full focus is an uncommon gift. The early morning, with its inborn tranquility and absence of interferences, permits us to completely give and get this gift. Without the ping of notices or the surge of timetables, we can really tune in and be available with each other, fortifying the obligations of closeness and trust.

Developing a Culture of Health

By remembering friends and family for our morning schedule, we support our connections as well as develop a culture of health inside our circle. Empowering and supporting each other in rehearses like reflection, work out, or careful eating establishes an aggregate vibe of wellbeing and prosperity. This common obligation to health can rouse and elevate all interested parties, making a positive expanding influence all through our more extensive local area.

The Groundbreaking Force of Custom

Changing these early collaborations into a custom pervades them with a feeling of importance and expectation. Over the long run, what might start as a basic common action turns into a loved part of our relationship, a wellspring of satisfaction and association that we anticipate every day. These ceremonies become the strings that weave the texture of our connections, implanting a profound feeling of having a place and fellowship in our lives.

In embracing the 5 AM hour, we carve out an opportunity for individual progression as well as a valuable chance to enhance our connections. Through shared quietness, discussion, and customs, we extend our associations with people around us, improving our aggregate prosperity and winding around a more tight snare of help and love. As we ascend with the sunrise, we do so as people chasing after our own development as well as accomplices, families, and companions, filling together in the calm excellence of the morning light.

CHAPTER 5: OVERCOMING CHALLENGES AND SETBACKS

Distinguishing Normal Snags

The excursion to embrace the 5 a.m. way of life isn't without its obstacles. Likewise, with any huge way of life change, taking on a standard that includes getting up early can introduce difficulties that may, on occasion, feel inconceivable. This part expects to shine a light on these normal deterrents, not to put you down but to set you up for the street ahead. Understanding these difficulties is the most vital step toward conquering them.

The Fight with the Morning Timer

The first and most clear test is the fight with the morning timer. For some, awakening while the other world dozes is overwhelming. The glow and solace of the bed at 5 AM can cause good motivations to appear to be ancient history. This battle isn't simply physical yet mental, as it sets our prompt craving for solace in opposition to our drawn-out objectives for self-improvement.

Consistency: The Tough Trip

Keeping up with consistency is another critical test. Life is erratic, and there will be days when adhering to a 5 a.m. reminder appears to be close to unthinkable. Whether because of late-night commitments, interferences with your rest, or basically an absence of inspiration, the capacity to remain steady is frequently tested.

Managing Interferences

Life doesn't interrupt us from our own objectives. Interferences to our daily practice, like travel, sickness, or family crises, can wreck our advancement. These interferences can be deterring, driving us to scrutinize our responsibility and capacity to keep up with our initial rising propensity.

The psychological obstacle

Past the physical and calculated difficulties lies a psychological obstacle. Questioning, apprehension about disappointment, and the solace of old propensities can cloud our determination. The psyche can be our most prominent partner or our most considerable foe in the journey to get up on time. Overcoming this psychological obstacle requires something beyond discipline; it requires a change in context.

Changing deterrents into potential open doors

Every deterrent presents a chance for development. The trouble of getting up early can show us our body's requirements and the significance of resting cleanliness. Battles with consistency feature the worth of tirelessness and the need to adjust our procedures to life's consistently evolving conditions. Interferences in our routine can test our flexibility and help us be adaptable in our methodology. In conclusion, the psychological obstacles we face help us remember the force of mentality in accomplishing our objectives.

By perceiving the truth about these difficulties—venturing stones instead of barricades—we can move toward them with a proactive outlook. This part of the book isn't just about distinguishing snags; it's tied in with furnishing you with the comprehension and point of view expected to actually explore them. The excursion to turning into a ray of sunshine in the morning is as much about defeating these difficulties as it's worth partaking in the serenity and efficiency of the early hours.

Methodologies for Keeping Up with Inspiration

Inspiration is the fuel that drives our excursion toward taking on a 5 a.m. way of life. Nonetheless, it's normal for this fuel to drain after some time, particularly when confronted with difficulties and misfortunes. To guarantee a consistent stock of inspiration, it is essential to embrace methodologies that keep the flares of energy consuming, in any event, when the oddity of getting up early fades or hindrances cloud our way.

Setting clear, reachable objectives

The foundation of supported inspiration is the setting of clear, reachable objectives. These objectives shouldn't simply be sufficiently aggressive to move, but also adequately reasonable to achieve. Separate your overall objective of taking on a 5 AM standard into more modest, reasonable achievements. Praise every accomplishment, regardless of how little, to create a feeling of progress and achievement. Keep in mind that getting up early is a long-distance race, not a run; it is vital to find a steady speed.

Tracking down Your Why

Understanding the reason why you need to get up at 5 AM is a strong inspiration. Is it to possess calm energy for yourself, to work out, to reflect, or to deal with a meaningful venture? Your "why" ought to reverberate with your own qualities and goals. At the point when your caution goes off in the early morning, it's this characteristic inspiration—the vision of the existence you're building—that will move you up.

Building a Steady People Group

People are innately friendly animals, and the help of a local area can fundamentally reinforce our inspiration. Associate with other people who share your objective of rising early. This can be through internet-based discussions, online entertainment gatherings, or neighborhood meetups. Sharing your encounters, difficulties, and victories with similar people creates a feeling of brotherhood and responsibility, making the excursion not so confining but rather more charming.

Imagining Achievement

Perception is an integral asset for keeping up with inspiration. Put in no time flat every day, envisioning yourself effectively getting up at 5 AM and participating in your morning schedule. Imagine the sensations of achievement and their positive effect on your day. This psychological practice primes your subliminal to line up with your cognizant objectives, making the early wake-up a piece of your self-personality.

Adjusting and Advancing Your Methodology

At last, be ready to adjust your methodology as you realize what turns out best for you. In the event that you find your inspiration melting away, reconsider your systems. Maybe you really want to change your sleep time, find new morning exercises that invigorate you, or change your nighttime schedule for better rest. The key is to see every day as a chance to learn and develop, not simply in that frame of mind to get up early, but in understanding yourself and what drives you.

By carrying out these systems, you fabricate a powerful structure for keeping up with inspiration. This section isn't just about getting up ahead of schedule; it's tied in with bridling the force of inspiration to change your mornings and, likewise, your life. With clear objectives, a solid why, local area backing, representation, and versatility, you'll track down the solidarity to defeat the dormancy of the comfortable bed and embrace the commitment of the early hours.

Adjusting to Life's Unusualness

The way toward laying out a 5 AM normal is cleared with good motivation. Nonetheless, life's inborn unusualness frequently messes up our all-around laid plans. Whether because of startling travel, an ailment, or huge life-altering situations, these disturbances can seem like inconceivable boundaries to our advancement. However, it is even with such unconventionality that our obligation to the 5 AM way of life is really tried and can be significantly reinforced.

Embracing Adaptability

The key to exploring life's unusual moments lies in adaptability. Unbending nature in our schedules can prompt disappointment and a feeling of disappointment when we definitely experience disturbances. All things being equal, embracing an adaptable methodology permits us to change our assumptions and techniques without forsaking our objectives. For example, in the event that disease makes it difficult to wake at 5 AM, changing our wake-up time briefly doesn't mean we've fizzled; rather, it implies a cognizant variation to our ebb and flow conditions.

Fostering an Emergency Course of Action

Having an emergency course of action set up for times when our routine is disturbed can have a tremendous effect. This could include distinguishing center components of your morning schedule that can be altered or abbreviated as opposed to skipped completely. For instance, a dense rendition of your morning exercise or contemplation meeting can keep up with the coherence of your normal in any event when time is restricted.

Versatility, Even with Change

Interruptions to our routine are not just snags; they are chances to develop strength. Each time we adjust our daily schedule because of life's changes, we fortify our capacity to stay focused on our objectives under shifting conditions. This versatility turns into the foundation of our morning routine as well as our way to deal with life's difficulties overall.

Getting Back to Schedule

Maybe the most basic part of managing interruptions is the capacity to get back to our routine once the prompt obstruction has passed. The straightforwardness with which we can continue our 5 AM reminders and related exercises is a demonstration of the strength of the propensities we've fabricated. It's critical to move toward this return with consideration and persistence, perceiving that getting once more into the musicality might take time.

An Illustration of Temporariness

Eventually, adjusting to life's unconventionality shows us a significant illustration of fleetingness and the significance of being available. Our capacity to change and push ahead, regardless of the recurring pattern of life's requests, enhances our excursion toward self-improvement. It builds up the possibility that the 5 AM unrest isn't just about the hour we wake, but about how we answer our general surroundings with beauty, adaptability, and flexibility.

Tackling the Impact of Trained Instinct Development

Understanding the study of propensity development is instrumental in beating the difficulties related to laying out a 5 AM standard. This information equips us with the devices to change our yearnings into programmed ways of behaving, making the early morning awakening a periodic triumph as well as a staple of our day-to-day routines.

The Life Structures of a Propensity

At its center, each propensity comprises three key parts: the prompt, the daily practice, and the prize. The sign triggers the way of behaving, the routine is the actual conduct, and the award is the advantage gotten from the way of behaving. With regards to a 5 AM awakening, the prompt may be the morning timer, the routine is the demonstration of rising early, and the prize could be the serenity and efficiency of the early morning hours.

Establishing a helpful climate

To offset the impact of trained instinct development, establishing a climate that upholds your initial wake-up goal is essential. This could mean setting your morning timer across the space to forestall napping, setting up your morning fundamentals the prior night, or laying out a loosening up sleep time custom that signals to your body that now is the ideal time to slow down. By adjusting your current circumstances to your objectives, you lessen the grinding associated with early rising, making it simpler to adhere to your daily practice.

Utilizing gradual changes

The excursion towards turning into a go-getter is many times more fruitful when moved toward through gradual changes as opposed to uncommon changes. Slowly setting your caution prior to 15-minute augmentations can facilitate the change and assist your body with acclimating to the new timetable. This calculated methodology lessens the shock to your framework, making the propensity more reasonable over the long haul.

The Job of Remunerations

Rewards assume a critical role in supporting new propensities. Distinguishing a prize that is significant and promptly satisfying can essentially expand your possibilities while adhering to your 5 AM standard. Whether it's the fulfillment of partaking in a tranquil mug of espresso in isolation or the additional time acquired for individual undertakings, finding your extraordinary prize is a strong inspiration.

Building an emotionally supportive network

At long last, the course of propensity development is often reinforced by a steady local area. Offering your objectives to companions, family, or a devoted gathering can give you the consolation and responsibility expected to drive forward. Praising achievements, but little, supports the positive parts of your new propensity, integrating it further into your day-to-day routine.

Basically, understanding and applying the standards of propensity development can change the test of getting up at 5 AM from an overwhelming errand into a characteristic and remunerating part of your day. By zeroing in on the prompts, schedules, and rewards that shape our way of behaving, we can methodically destroy the hindrances to early rising, making ready for a more useful and satisfying way of life.

Embracing the Excursion of Self-Disclosure

The last and maybe most significant point in defeating difficulties and misfortunes as you focus on getting up at 5 AM is the excursion of self-revelation it starts. This excursion rises above the simple activity of setting a caution or making a morning schedule; it turns into an intelligent investigation of what your identity is, what you are worth, and how you wish to spend the valuable hours of your life.

Self-Reflection and Development

The calm of the early morning offers an unequaled chance for self-reflection. At these times, liberated from the interruptions and requests of the day, you can genuinely pay attention to your internal voice. This time for thoughtfulness can prompt critical self-improvement as you recognize your objectives and goals as well as the obstructions, both external and internal, that have frustrated your advancement. The 5 AM Transformation isn't just about switching your wake-around time; it's tied in with looking at your life from a perspective of lucidity and expectation.

Figuring out your why

The key to the excursion of self-disclosure is figuring out your 'why'—the main thrust behind your choice to embrace the 5 AM way of life. This understanding goes past shallow inspirations, venturing into the profundities of your own qualities and desires. Maybe you look for additional opportunity for imagination, a craving to work on your wellbeing, or the need to discover a sense of reconciliation in a turbulent world. Whatever your reason, it turns into the reference point that guides you through dim mornings and troublesome times.

Developing versatility and adaptability

The most common way of adjusting to another daily practice, particularly one that includes getting up essentially sooner than you're familiar with, normally develops strength and adaptability. These characteristics are significant, not simply in the frame of mind of your morning schedule, but in all everyday issues. As you explore the difficulties of the 5 AM Transformation, you figure out how to move toward mishaps with a critical thinking mentality, seeing them as any open doors for learning and development as opposed to unconquerable snags.

The Compensations of Determination

The compensations of your determination reach out a long way past the underlying fulfillment of vanquishing the nap button. They manifest in expanded efficiency, a more profound feeling of harmony, and an elevated consciousness of your life's direction and reason. This groundbreaking excursion reshapes your mornings as well as your whole way of dealing with life, implanting a feeling of direction and deliberateness in all that you do.

A Consistent Excursion

At last, the excursion of self-disclosure started at 5 a.m. Insurgency is nonstop. Every morning presents another amazing chance to find out about yourself, to refine your schedules, and to adjust your activities to your most profound qualities. Embracing this excursion with receptiveness and interest prompts a more extravagant, seriously satisfying life, set apart by a significant association with your own true capacity.

All in all, the 5 AM Transformation offers significantly more than a basic change in awakened time; it is an entryway to self-revelation, self-awareness, and a more purposeful approach to everyday life. By conquering difficulties and misfortunes with versatility, adaptability, and a profound comprehension of your why, you open your true capacity for the day ahead as well as for your life all in all.

CONCLUSION: THE JOURNEY AHEAD

Thinking about the change

As we arrive at the end of our excursion together, it's fundamental to stop and ponder the significant change you've gone through by embracing the 5 a.m. upheaval. This excursion was rarely pretty much getting up right on time; it was tied in with opening a way to your true capacity, each morning in turn. You've set out in a way that has reshaped your mornings, reclassified your efficiency, and, in particular, revived your healthy identity.

Recognizing Your Development

From the primary speculative strides of adjusting your wake-up opportunity to completely coordinating this new mood into your life, you've exhibited wonderful development. This development isn't estimated only by the undertakings you've achieved before first light yet by the further comprehension you've acquired about the main thing to you. The discipline expected to ascend with the sun has saturated different parts of your life, empowering you to move toward difficulties with a steadier hand and a more clear brain.

The Effect on Efficiency and Prosperity

Your efficiency has likely seen a critical lift, not on the grounds that you've basically added a couple of additional hours to your day, but since you've figured out how to purposefully utilize your time more. Nonetheless, the advantages reach out a long way past efficiency measurements. The tranquil isolation of the early morning has offered you a safe haven for reflection, prompting an upgraded feeling of prosperity. This time has turned into a hallowed space for you to sustain your psychological, close-to-home, and actual well-being, establishing an inspirational vibe that helps through the remainder of your day.

Valuing the Progressions

The progressions you've encountered may have come progressively, making them barely noticeable. Pause for a minute to see the value in how far you've come. Recall the individual you were prior to leaving on this excursion. Ponder the snapshots of battle, the mornings when the glow of your bed appeared to be a fantastic rival, and perceive the strength you've displayed in conquering these difficulties. Commend the triumphs, regardless of how little they appear, for they are the building blocks of your changed life.

An Establishment for Future Development

This change isn't an end, but an establishment whereupon you can keep on building. The propensities you've created, the discipline you've developed, and the experiences you've acquired about yourself are instruments that will work well for you as you seek after future objectives. The 5 AM Upset has not quite recently changed your mornings; it has furnished you with a mentality that can change each part of your life.

As you ponder the excursion you've embraced, recall that every day carries another chance to build up these changes, to drive yourself further, and to advance. The genuine force of the 5 AM transformation lies not in the actual hour but rather in the individual you become by embracing it.

Supporting Your 5 AM Upheaval

With the establishment set and the underlying change in progress, the inquiry currently goes to manageability. How would you guarantee that this insurgency, this recently discovered way to deal with mornings and life, turns into an extremely durable installation as opposed to a temporary investigation? The critical lies in understanding that the 5 AM Upset is certainly not an unbending arrangement of rules but rather an adaptable, living practice that adjusts to the developing forms of your life.

Adjusting to Life's Progressions

Life is a powerful excursion, loaded up with unforeseen turns, difficulties, and stages. Accordingly, your way to deal with the 5 AM standard must likewise be dynamic, equipped for flexing to oblige life's unavoidable changes. Whether it's a change in your work, relational peculiarities, wellbeing, or essentially an adjustment of seasons, the pith of your morning schedule ought to stay in one piece regardless of whether the particulars should be changed. Embrace these changes not as misfortunes but rather as open doors to refine and advance your training.

Remaining Spurred

Inspiration can disappear after the underlying fervor blurs. To balance this, help yourself routinely remember the advantages you've encountered from rising early. Keep a diary of your achievements, but keep it small, and survey it when your purpose starts to slip. Laying out new objectives and difficulties for your morning hours can likewise infuse new energy into your daily schedule. Keep in mind that the 5 AM Upheaval is an excursion of individual investigation and development, and there is, in every case, a new landscape to find.

Consistent objective setting

Objectives provide bearing and motivation for your initial mornings. As you accomplish your underlying objectives, set new ones to keep your mornings testing and fulfilling. These objectives ought not be restricted to efficiency or profession, but ought to likewise include self-improvement, wellbeing, connections, and leisure activities. By consistently laying out and seeking after new objectives, you guarantee that your mornings remain a period of significant commitment to yourself and your desires.

Integrating Responsibility

One of the best ways to support your 5 a.m. normal is to consolidate components of responsibility. This could be a similar local area, a 5 AM club, or even a companion or relative who shares your obligation to self-awareness. Checking in with your responsibility partner(s) can provide both the support and the delicate tension expected to remain focused.

Reflecting and celebrating

Routinely find the opportunity to think about your excursion and praise your advancement. Recognizing and commending the achievements you reach builds up your obligation to the 5 AM way of life. Whether it's denoting the commemoration of your 5 a.m. start date or commending a specific objective accomplished during these early hours, these snapshots of reflection and festivity are pivotal for supporting your inspiration and responsibility.

In supporting your 5 AM Upset, remember that adaptability, diligence, and an emphasis on nonstop development are your most noteworthy partners. By adjusting to life's changes, remaining roused, defining new objectives, consolidating responsibility, and finding opportunity to reflect and commend, you can guarantee that your initial morning unrest stays a lively and remunerating part of your life.

Embracing People Groups and Sharing Your Excursion

As you harden your obligation to the 5 AM Upset, an important system for keeping up with your energy is to draw in a local area of similar people. This commitment can change your single process into a common experience, loaded with help, motivation, and aggregate insight. The force acts independently, giving you an organization of consolation and responsibility that pushes you forward.

Tracking down your clan

In the period of computerized networks, finding a local area of go-getters is more open than at any time in recent memory. Online discussions, web-based entertainment gatherings, and virtual meet-ups offer stages where people from across the globe share their encounters, difficulties, and victories connected with getting up ahead of schedule and boosting their mornings. Joining such a gathering can furnish you with the feeling of having a place and a repository of inspiration and guidance. On the other hand, you could find or make a nearby gathering with individuals who meet truly to share systems, partake in early morning exercises, or basically partake in the calm of the day break together.

Sharing Your Encounters

Imparting your excursion to others can be both therapeutic and edifying. It offers you an opportunity to ponder your advancement, articulate your difficulties, and praise your triumphs. In doing so, you not only add clarity and viewpoint to your own process but additionally give support and knowledge to other people. The demonstration of sharing creates a criticism circle of help and discovery that benefits both the provider and the collector.

Gaining from the System

Each individual's 5 AM venture is special, loaded up with customized ceremonies, obstructions, and wins. Drawing in with a local area permits you to gain from the different encounters of others. This aggregate insight can be a rich asset for conquering your own challenges and tracking down new systems to upgrade your morning schedule. Whether it's a clever way to deal with using time effectively, a proposal for a care practice, or guidance for offsetting early mornings with everyday life, the local area offers a gold mine of information.

The Strength of Responsibility

Past inspiration and counsel, a local area gives a strong responsibility component. Realizing that others are depending on you to share your advancement or that you have a registration can be a convincing motivation to adhere to your 5 AM responsibility, even on mornings when the compulsion to hit nap areas of strength is. This responsibility can take many forms, from formal concurrences with responsibility accomplices to relaxed registrations inside a gathering. The key is that this outside assumption adds an extra layer of obligation to your own objectives.

Extending Your Effect

As you become more knowledgeable about your 5 AM venture, you have the valuable chance to coach other people who are simply starting their way. Sharing your experiences, tips, and consolation can assist rookies with exploring their initial difficulties all the more easily. In doing so, you improve the excursion of others as well as support your own responsibility and comprehension of the 5 AM Transformation. Educating and coaching can be integral assets for self-improvement, establishing your own practices while helping other people to reach their true potential.

Embracing people groups and sharing your process adds a rich social aspect to the 5 AM Upset. It changes the training from a singular undertaking into an aggregate development where backing, learning, and shared responsibility flourish. By tracking down your clan, sharing your encounters, gaining from the group, utilizing the strength of responsibility, and extending your effect through mentorship, you can support and develop your obligation to rise early and live purposefully.

Utilizing Innovation for Consistency

In the pursuit of supporting the 5 AM Unrest, innovation assumes an urgent role in improving consistency and guaranteeing that your initial mornings are a propensity as well as a way of life. The prudent utilization of innovation can smooth out your morning schedule, assisting you with keeping focused, measuring progress, and keeping up with the discipline important to early receiving the rewards of rising.

Savvy Cautions for a Delicate Wake-Up

The most vital phase in an effective 5 AM awakening is, normally, awakening. Savvy caution applications and gadgets offer functionalities a long way past customary alerts, including highlights that copy the dawn and slowly expanding light and sound to wake you all the more normally and delicately. These innovations can fundamentally improve the nature of your morning awakening, making it simpler to rise early and reliably without the shock to your framework that a boisterous, sudden caution can cause.

Following and Investigating the Rest

Understanding and streamlining your rest designs is vital to supporting early wake-up times. Rest following applications and wearables give itemized experiences into your rest cycles, span, and quality. By dissecting this information, you can change your sleep time schedules, rest climate, and, surprisingly, your eating regimen to work on the nature of your rest. Better rest quality guarantees that you awaken feeling revived and prepared to embrace the capabilities of your initial morning hours.

Booking and Errand The board devices

When you're up, having an unmistakable arrangement for your morning can essentially expand your efficiency and guarantee that you capitalize on these early hours. Tasks on the board and planning applications permit you to frame your morning standard, set boundaries, and keep tabs on your development over the long run. Whether it's devoting time to work out, reflecting, perusing, or dealing with individual ventures, these instruments can assist you with building an organized and effective morning schedule.

Propensity to Follow Applications

Consistency is key to making the 5 AM Unrest an enduring piece of your life. Propensity following applications are intended to help you assemble and keep up with positive routines by giving visual advancement following, updates, and inspirational prizes. By following your consistency in getting up at 5 AM and finishing your planned morning exercises, these applications can build up your responsibility and give you a feeling of achievement.

Getting to an Uplifting and Instructive Substance

At long last, utilizing innovation to get to helpful and instructive substances can increase inspiration and learning. Webcasts, book recordings, and online courses can transform your morning hours into a period for self-awareness and development. Whether it's learning another dialect, investigating philosophical ideas, or standing by and listening to persuasive discussions, innovation can carry a universe of information to your fingertips, improving your initial morning experience.

By integrating these innovative devices into your 5 AM standard, you can improve your capacity to get up right on time, streamline your rest, plan and execute a useful morning schedule, track your propensities, and draw in content that moves and teaches. Innovation, when utilized nicely, turns into a strong partner in your journey to support the 5 AM Upheaval, assisting you with building a morning schedule that isn't just reliable yet, in addition to improving and aligning with your self-awareness objectives.

Observing Advancement and Embracing Adaptability

As you think about the excursion of the 5 AM Insurgency, it's fundamental to perceive the headway you've made and the versatility you've constructed. This last point highlights the significance of commending your triumphs, but little, and embracing the adaptability expected to support this extraordinary propensity over the long haul. It's an update that the way to self-improvement isn't straight yet, but a progression of rhythmic movements that, when explored with effortlessness, lead to significant self-disclosure and accomplishment.

Observing Little Wins

Each day that you ascend at 5 a.m. and devote time to your self-awareness is a triumph. It's essential to recognize these minutes, praising the discipline and exertion it takes to keep up with this daily practice. Whether it's through journaling your achievements, imparting achievements to companions or a care group, or essentially pausing for a minute to ponder your development, perceiving your advancement powers your inspiration and builds up the worth of your initial morning responsibility.

Gaining from Misfortunes

The excursion will unavoidably incorporate misfortunes. There will be days when the glow of your bed keeps you down or life's erratic requests infringe on your initial hours. As opposed to reviewing these minutes as disappointments, consider them to be amazing chances to learn and adjust. Think about what prompted the misfortune and consider changes in accordance with your daily schedule or attitude that can assist you with conquering comparative difficulties later on. The strength gained through exploring these hindrances is important in showing you your cutoff points and how to push past them delicately.

Embracing Adaptability

While the 5 AM Upheaval is based on consistency, adaptability is vital to its drawn-out manageability. Life's liabilities and your own necessities will advance, expecting adjustments to how you approach your initial mornings. Adaptability could mean changing your wake-up time on specific days to accommodate rest or altering your morning schedule to reflect changing objectives and interests. The capacity to adjust while keeping up with the embodiment of your initial morning responsibility is a demonstration of the transformation's reconciliation into your life.

Coordinating Criticism and Changing Objectives

As you progress, consistently look for input from your own encounters and potentially from others to refine your methodology. This could include tweaking your rest plan, exploring different avenues regarding different morning exercises, or changing your assumptions to line up with your world. The objective isn't inflexible adherence to a set arrangement, but rather a developing excursion that best serves your development and prosperity.

Looking Forward with Idealism

At long last, view your excursion from the perspective of confidence. The 5 AM Unrest isn't just about the hours you guarantee before the day starts; it's about the individual you become all the while. With each early morning, you're laying the groundwork of discipline, care, and efficiency that reaches out a long way past the clock. Celebrate where you are, anticipate where you're going, and recall that every day carries another chance to mold your existence with expectation and reason.

All things being equal, the 5 AM Upheaval is in excess of a propensity; a groundbreaking excursion offers significant experiences into your capacities, wants, and the existence you wish to make. By commending your advancement, gaining from mishaps, embracing adaptability, incorporating criticism, and looking forward with good faith, you furnish yourself with the versatility and flexibility fundamental for supported development. Allow every morning to be a step in the right direction in your excursion, loaded up with the commitment of disclosure and the potential for significance.

APPENDICES

Appendix A: Recommended Reading and Resources

To develop your comprehension and improve your excursion with the 5 AM Revolution, the accompanying books and assets are strongly suggested. They cover a scope of points from efficiency and using time effectively to prosperity and self-awareness.

Books:

"The Miracle Morning" by Hal Elrod - A transformative guide to how waking up early can dramatically improve your life.

"Atomic Habits" by James Clear - Offers a comprehensive look at the science of habits and how small changes can lead to remarkable results.

"Mindfulness in Plain English" by Bhante Henepola Gunaratana - A practical guide to developing mindfulness and meditation practices.

"Deep Work" by Cal Newport - Explores the benefits of focused work and how to achieve more in less time.

"The 4-Hour Workweek" by Timothy Ferriss - Challenges conventional work norms and offers insights on productivity and lifestyle design.

Online Resources:

The 5 AM Club Community: Online forums and groups where individuals practicing the 5 AM lifestyle share tips, challenges, and successes.

Headspace or Calm: Meditation apps that offer guided sessions to help start your morning with mindfulness.

Evernote or Notion: Note-taking apps that can be used for journaling, planning your day, or tracking habits.

Appendix B: Templates and Checklists for Your 5 AM Routine

To assist you in implementing and maintaining your 5 AM routine, the following templates and checklists are provided:

1. **Morning Routine Template:**
   Wake-Up Time:
   Hydration:
   Exercise/Physical Activity:
   Meditation/Mindfulness Practice:
   Goal Setting/Planning for the Day:
   Personal Development (Reading/Writing):
2. **Habit Tracker:**
   Use this to mark each day you successfully complete your 5 AM routine, including specific activities you've committed to.
3. **Weekly Reflection Template:**

Achievements of the Week:
Lessons Learned:
Adjustments for Next Week:
Checklists:
Preparing for Your Morning the Night Before
Essential Elements of a Productive Morning
Weekly Planning and Review Checklist

Appendix C: FAQs About the 5 AM Lifestyle

Q1: Is waking up at 5 AM suitable for everyone? A1: While the 5 AM lifestyle has many benefits, it's important to consider individual differences. Listen to your body and adapt the concept to fit your personal health needs and lifestyle.

Q2: What if I fail to wake up at 5 AM consistently? A2: It's normal to face challenges initially. Focus on consistency rather than perfection, and gradually adjust your sleep schedule to make waking up at 5 AM more manageable.

Q3: How do I prevent burnout with a 5 AM routine? A3: Ensure your morning routine includes time for self-care and relaxation. Balance productivity with activities that nourish your well-being to prevent burnout.

Q4: Can I adjust the 5 AM routine to fit my schedule? A4: Absolutely. The core idea is to dedicate the first hours of your day to personal growth and productivity. If 5 AM is too early due to your circumstances, adjust the time to suit your schedule while maintaining the essence of the practice.

Q5: How long does it take to see benefits from waking up at 5 AM? A5: The timeline varies for each individual, but many report noticing improvements in productivity, mood, and overall well-being within the first few weeks of consistently practicing the 5 AM routine.

These appendices are designed to provide you with additional support and guidance as you embark on or continue your journey with the 5 AM Revolution. By leveraging these resources, templates, and FAQs, you'll be well-equipped to optimize your mornings and unlock your full potential, one morning at a time.